Close Up Of A Honeybee

Virgil E. Foster

Close-Up Of A Honeybee

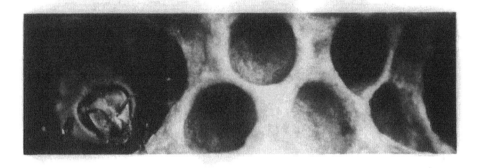

By Virgil E. Foster

Photographed by Martin Iger

NEW YORK: YOUNG SCOTT BOOKS

To Ann Foster

Close-Up Of A Honeybee

PART ONE:

Adventure On The Beach

One summer when I took my vacation at the seashore, I had an interesting experience. This is the story of that experience.

I was walking along the beach one day, picking up a few sea shells, when it happened.

I saw a lovely big white shell near the foamy edge of the water and when I bent down to pick it up I noticed some wet sand moving up and down. What could be making the sand jump like that? Could it be a crab?

I watched closely. Soon I saw something that looked like two little legs pushing up through the wet sand. Then something that looked like a tiny pair of pincers came between them. Whatever was buried in the sand was trying hard to get out. Maybe I could help it.

I scooped up the moving sand in the big white shell and put it on a board that I found near by.

When I gently pushed away some of the sand, I saw a strange little blob that seemed to be struggling to get out. At first it did not look like anything I had ever seen. But soon six legs kicked and pushed more sand away, and a body began to appear. Now I could see that it was a bee.

It stopped moving. It was so still that I thought it must be dead. But, I was wrong.

It *was* moving. It began to twist and turn.

It rolled over onto its feet.

The poor bee! It was wet all over and weighted down with sand. It must have been flying near the water when a big wave caught it and washed it under the sand.

One wing seemed to be missing. I wondered if it had been broken off. Just as I was thinking that the bee could never fly again with only one wing . . .

. . . the other wing popped up. Now the bee might be able to
fly again if it could get all that wet, sticky sand off.

And that is just what the bee began to do. It sat up on its tail and got busy with all of its six legs, brushing the wet grains of sand off its body and out of its hair.

It worked so hard that it almost fell over. Now I could see what looked like a tongue curled back under its head. What a big tongue for such a little bee!

The bee tried again and again to get the sand out of the hair on top of its head. I decided to help it. I found a blade of grass and carefully flipped off some of the sand. The bee seemed surprised. It backed away a little but then went on with its cleaning.

Oops! . . . The bee cleaned so hard that it seemed to lose its balance.

But no, it hadn't lost its balance. The bee was using its tongue as a brace while it cleaned its delicate wings with its hind legs.

Then, using its two front legs, it cleaned its tongue carefully.

Finally it kicked away the last little grain of sand and I could see clearly that it was a honeybee. Now it was all clean, but the hair on its back was still wet.

For several minutes, the honeybee sat quietly in the sun-
shine until it was completely dry and fluffy. Then it flew away.

I stood there for a while. Then I walked slowly along the beach, thinking about what I had seen. I had never paid much attention to bees before. But after watching this one I wanted to know more about them. I wondered if ever again I would have such an interesting experience with a bee.

PART TWO:

Rescue and Revival

A few days later I did have another experience with honeybees.

I was staying in a cottage that had some cracks between one wall and the roof. Each night several bees came in through the cracks. In the morning they flew to a window and tried to get out. They tried over and over again until finally they dropped to the floor and died. One morning I watched the last bee crawl up the windowpane. It stopped as if it were tired, then suddenly . . .

. . . it dropped to the floor and lay still. Was it dead? I got down on my knees and looked closely but I wasn't sure. Maybe this bee needed help too. Maybe it was just too tired to keep trying to find its way outdoors. Maybe it was hungry. I rolled the bee onto a piece of paper, carried it outside, and put it on the path. The bee still did not move.

I knew that bees get their food from the nectar of flowers, so I picked a flower and put it down in front of the bee. What do you suppose happened?

Almost at once the bee struggled to its feet, walked right over to the flower, and reached up to it.

It climbed up on the flower and pushed its head between the petals, searching for nectar. It must have been very hungry.

Finally the bee found the nectar and began to draw it up so hard that its body shook. It was busy eating and paid no attention to me. I got up close enough to watch. Its wings were very thin and I could see the light and dark bands of the bee's body right through them.

As the bee ate, it spread its wings. I was surprised to see that there were four—two wings on each side. I had always thought that a honeybee had only two wings, like a bird.

At last the bee seemed to have eaten all the food it needed. It rested awhile and then flew away.

Seeing the "dead" bee come to life again and fly away made me feel good. I was glad that I had been able to help it.

I wondered about the other "dead" bees on the floor. Could they be revived too? And, if I could revive a bee with a flower, could I do it even better with honey?

I found a jar of honey in the kitchen and dipped a little of it onto a spoon. Then I rolled another bee from the floor onto a piece of paper. I carried it to the porch and put a big drop of honey near its head.

The bee looked at the honey and used what little strength
it had to drag itself close to the honey so that it could eat.

After eating a little honey, the bee struggled to its feet.

It looked weak and its legs wobbled, but it stood up and waded right into the honey.

The bee stayed in the honey quite awhile, drawing honey through its tongue. Then it backed out. But its legs, tongue, and the hair on the lower part of its body were all gooey. So it began to clean off the honey. It went through the same motions as the bee I had watched on the beach. When it was clean again, the bee rested awhile and then flew away.

Some of the bees on the floor were really dead. But I revived as many as I could and turned them loose to fly away.

After reviving all the exhausted bees that morning, I caught and rescued those that were still on the windowpane trying to get out. As a bee crawled up the window I held a drinking glass against the window above it. Since the bee always crawled up the window, it crawled right into the glass. Then I put a piece of paper over the top of the glass, went outdoors, and let the bee fly away.

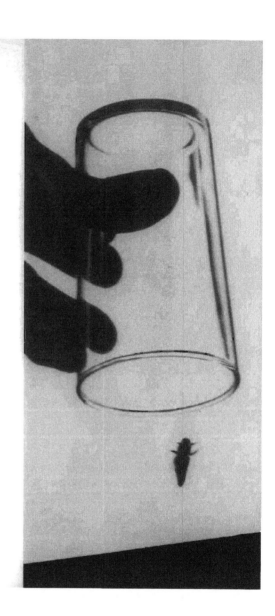

PART THREE:

Honeybees Up Close

Watching the bees come to life again was so interesting that I wanted to learn more about them. I bought a magnifying glass and borrowed some books about bees from the library.

Every morning, when I caught a bee in a glass, I looked at it through the magnifying glass and read about what I was seeing.

One of the things I learned from the books was that all the bees I had seen were female honeybees, called *worker* bees, or *field* bees.

I had noticed that a honeybee's six legs and her four wings are all attached to the middle section of her body. Back of this section is the tail section, which is very interesting to see through a magnifying glass. It has golden-yellow and dark-brown bands around it and lies in folds so that it can bend. Between these folds on the underside of the tail section are wax glands. From these wax glands comes the beeswax which the bees use to make the honeycomb for their hives.

On each side of the bee's head is a large compound eye which can see in many directions at once. These eyes are covered with tiny hairs. The two thin things sticking out of the front of the bee's head are *antennae* that the bee uses for feeling and smelling.

I watched many bees through my magnifying glass as they crawled around over the flowers I gave them. In addition to her two large eyes, a honeybee has three small eyes on top of her head. These eyes help her find her way. You can see one of these little eyes in this picture.

The honeybee's jaws move sideways instead of up and down. They are called *mandibles*. They are hard and dark, and the bee uses them to clip pollen from blossoms.

Just above and in front of these mandibles, or jaws, is a lip called a *labrum*, with which the bee tastes.

A honeybee has two tongues—a short, wide one and a long, thin one. The short tongue is in four pieces which come together to form a tube. The bee uses this short tongue to draw up nectar that is easy to reach.

The long, slender tongue is shaped at the end like a spoon. The bee uses this tongue for reaching deeper into flowers.

When the bee is not using her tongues, she rolls them back under her head the way an elephant curls up its trunk.

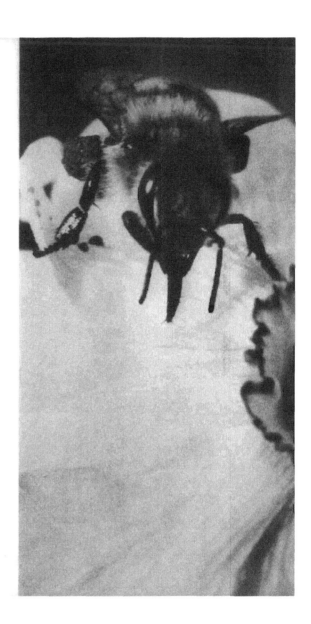

The honeybee's four wings interested me. Sometimes it was clear that there were two wings on each side. But at other times the two wings fitted together and looked like one.

The back edge of the front wing and the front edge of the back wing can hook together. When the honeybee needs to fly she hooks the two wings on each side together so that they act as one wing. When she has to go into a hive or into a blossom, she unhooks the wings and folds them over her back.

The more I learned about bees, the more I wanted to see how they live and work. I decided to visit a beehive.

PART FOUR:

The Hive and The Honey

I heard of a man who kept honeybees as a hobby, and I went to see him. When I told the beekeeper of my interest in bees, he said he would be glad to show me his beehives.

The beekeeper told me that wild honeybees make their homes in hollow trees or live under the roofs of old buildings or in the branches of trees. All honeybees used to have to find their own homes, but now beekeepers make hives for them. In hives bees have a better place to live and store their food. Sometimes a beekeeper can capture a wild colony of bees and put it into a hive. Or he can buy a few bees and put them into a hive to start a new colony.

Honeybees usually store more honey than they need. This extra honey is good food for people, and it is easier for the keeper to get this extra honey from a hive than from a bee tree or old house.

Beekeepers can put their beehives near orchards, clover fields, or other places where there are plenty of blossoms. With their food near by, the bees can make more honey than they could if they had to fly long distances to find blossoms.

The beekeeper gave me a hat with a veil hanging down around it. "This will keep the bees away from your face," he said. He had another hat like the one he gave me, and a strange-looking can with a bellows on the side of it. He called the can a *smoke pot*.

As we came near the hives, he put his hat on the ground and the smoke pot on a rock. He folded some corrugated paper and put it into the pot. Then he struck a match and lit it. The paper burned slowly and smoked. "I want to be sure the bees don't sting us," he said. "Honeybees have stingers in their tails. If you frighten or anger them, they will sting you. But the smoke will quiet them. I'll show you how it works."

The beekeeper put on his hat and veil and a pair of gloves. He went to a hive and gently lifted the cover.

Then he squeezed the bellows on the smoke pot and pumped a little smoke into the hive. "When the bees smell the smoke," he said, "they think their hive is burning. They rush into the hive and eat all the honey their stomachs will hold. A full stomach makes a bee lazy and less likely to sting."

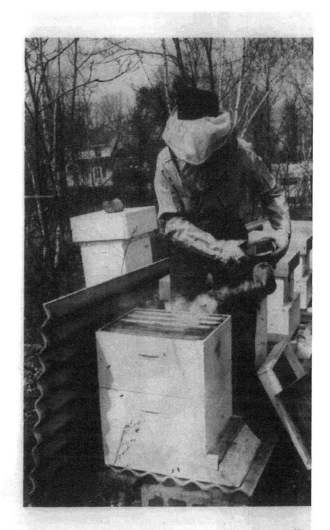

The keeper looked into the hive. "Now it is all right for you to come up close and see the bees," he said.

Some of the bees came out of the frames. But they were quiet and did not try to sting us.

"Now I'll show you one of the honey-combs," said the keeper. He took hold of a frame with a special clamp that worked like pincers. He lifted the frame out of the hive.

The keeper held up the frame and its honeycomb. "I never saw a honeycomb with bees on it," I said.

"Some of these cells have eggs in them. We call them *brood cells*. Around them are cells in which pollen has been stored. The pollen will be fed to the young bees in the cells. Near the edge of the comb are cells in which the bees store honey for use as food while they work in the hive.

"The bees can make their own honeycombs from beeswax, but that takes lots of time. I want the bees to spend as much time as possible making honey. So I put into each frame a comb foundation of manufactured wax, on which the bees build the walls of the cells."

The keeper took another frame out of the hive and looked at it.

"Here she is—the *queen* of the hive," he said. He took a little stick from his pocket and pointed to a bee that was longer than the others.

I looked at the queen through my magnifying glass.

"See her long body and small wings?" asked the keeper.

"Now look at a worker bee. Her body is much smaller than the queen's, but her wings are larger. The worker has strong wings because she flies much more than the queen and has to carry heavy loads."

"Each hive has several male bees too," added the keeper. "Male bees are called *drones*. Their only purpose is to fertilize the queen. A drone is larger than a worker bee but not as long as a queen."

"Is there only one queen in each hive?" I asked.

"Usually there is only one," the keeper answered. "But once in awhile—for a short time—there are two queens, an old queen and a young queen.

"Worker bees gather around the queen to protect her and feed her. They take care of all her needs."

"The queen is very important to the hive. She lays all the eggs from which new bees are hatched. In one year she may lay as many as two hundred thousand eggs.

"The queen lives in the two bottom sections of the hive, which we call *brood chambers*. Above them I put a *queen excluder* to keep the queen from getting into the upper sections and laying eggs in the combs in which I want the workers to store honey.

"A queen usually lives for two or three years. When she grows too old to lay as many eggs as are needed, the workers know they need a new queen. They secrete a special food from glands in their heads. We call it *royal jelly*. The workers give this royal jelly to several very young bees still in their cells. It makes them develop into queens. Without it they would become worker bees. When one new queen comes out of her cell before the others, she cuts a hole in each of the other queen cells and kills the other queens. A colony needs only one new queen. Sometimes two or more queens come out of their cells at the same time. They fight until only one is alive. She becomes the new queen.

"In midsummer a colony may have as many as fifty thousand bees living in one hive. Sometimes a colony becomes too large for one hive. Then the workers develop a new queen, and about half of the colony forms what we call a *swarm* with the new queen. They leave the hive to find a new home. I always keep an extra hive near by, and as soon as I see a swarm I put it into this hive before it can fly away. The more bees I have, the more honey they make."

"Do worker bees do anything besides gather nectar?" I asked the keeper.

"Young worker bees spend about the first three weeks of their lives in the hive as *house* bees," he answered. "House bees feed the queen and the young bees. They clean the hive. They prepare the cells for storing food and for the eggs the queen will lay.

"See the bees coming and going through the opening at the bottom of this hive! They are field bees. Most of them are leaving the hive to search for food. A few are coming into the hive. They are bringing in two kinds of food—nectar and pollen.

"The nectar that a field bee gathers is the sweet juice that is down inside of blossoms. Pollen, on the other hand, is a yellowish powder that you see in the center of a blossom.

"The house bees store the pollen and make the nectar into honey.

"The house bees chew the nectar, swallow it, force it out, and chew it again. They do this many times, until most of the water in the nectar evaporates. Then they store the honey in cells, where the rest of the water is allowed to evaporate. When the water has evaporated, the house bees build caps of wax over the honey to seal it in the cells.

"After serving for about three weeks as a house bee, the worker is strong enough to go into the fields and orchards to gather food. Then she becomes a field bee.

"When a field bee draws nectar from a blossom, she carries it in a special stomach called a *honey sac* until she gets back to the hive. As the bee goes in and out of blossoms, some of the pollen sticks to her body.

"She also gathers pollen by biting it loose with her mandibles or jaws. Then she carries the pollen to the hive to be stored in cells and to be fed to the queen and young bees."

"How does the bee carry the pollen back to the hive?" I asked.

"See the ball on this bee's hind leg? One section of each hind leg has a little hollow, like a basket. The bee packs the pollen into this basket. The *pollen basket* is also called a *breadbasket*, because pollen is often called *bee bread*.

"Sometimes a bee gathers only nectar. Sometimes she gathers only pollen. Often she gathers both. This bee has her tongue out as if she is gathering nectar as well as pollen."

Just then the keeper called my attention to a field bee that had alighted on a twig near by, probably to rest before going into the hive. Her breadbaskets were filled with balls of pollen almost as big as her head.

We went near enough to one of the beehives to watch the
bees coming in from the fields and orchards with their loads
of nectar and pollen.

A honeybee was crawling on my jacket. I didn't notice her and brushed my hand against her. She stung my hand. "Ouch!" I yelled.

"Don't move," called the keeper, "and don't touch it. Let me have your magnifying glass."

The keeper looked at my hand through the glass. "See? There is the bee's stinger and poison sac. When a honeybee stings you, she cannot pull out her stinger because it has barbs on it. When she pulls away, her stinger and poison sac are torn from her body. This kills her.

"Muscles in the poison sac keep working and force the poison through the stinger into your hand. Don't squeeze the poison sac in trying to get the stinger out, for that will only force more poison into your hand."

The keeper picked up another bee. She tried to sting him, but he held her so that her stinger could not reach him. I could see the stinger as she pushed it out.

"Don't *you* try to pick up a bee. A honeybee will sting you if she is angry or thinks you are going to hurt her or her hive. It is safer not to go near a beehive unless you are with a bee-keeper who knows how to handle bees," the keeper warned.

I wanted to know more about the bees. "You told me that a queen lives for several years. Does a worker bee live that long?" I asked.

"Not nearly that long," he replied. "During the busiest part of the summer, when there is a great deal of work to be done, a worker lives only about six weeks. But during the fall, when there isn't much nectar or pollen to gather, a worker doesn't wear herself out so fast and may live two or three times as long. Some of the bees hatched in the late fall live through the winter and help get the colony started again in the spring. All winter, when there is no pollen or nectar in the fields and orchards, they live on honey and pollen that have been stored in the cells."

"In this comb you see two groups of cells that are filled.
Those with the light-colored caps have honey in them. The
others are filled with pollen."

59

"What keeps them from freezing during a cold winter?" I asked. "Are the hives heated?"

"One of the most marvelous things about honeybees," the keeper said, "is the way they keep the hive warm during cold weather and cool in hot weather.

"When it is cold, bees keep warm by staying close together. Their body heat warms them and the hive. But what they do when the hive becomes hot is even more interesting.

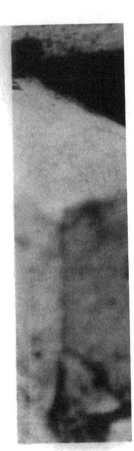

"See these bees? They are air-conditioning the hive. When it gets too hot, some bees line up at the entrance facing in, and fan their wings. This draws the hot air out of the hive. Cooler air then comes in through the cracks between sections of the hive. If there is a second opening, other bees go to it, face outward, and fan their wings to help bring cooler air into the hive. Their wings move so fast that you cannot even see them.

"If it is very hot, the bees do even more to cool the hive. They carry water into the hive, spread it on the combs, and then fan it so that evaporation cools the combs."

Imagine! Honeybees air-condition their houses!

There is much more to be learned about honeybees than I have told you. I hope that my story will help you to make your own discoveries about bees and other wonderful things in the world. One little bee opened to me a new world of nature. Perhaps she will open a door of adventure to you.

If You Want To Know More About Honeybees

you can find many articles and books about them in libraries and bookstores. The following are only a few to help you continue your adventure with bees.

"Inside The World Of The Honeybee," by Treat Davidson, is an excellent article in *The National Geographic Magazine* for August, 1959. It is illustrated with thirty-four colored pictures taken by the author.

THE FIRST BOOK OF BEES, by Albert B. Tibbets, is illustrated with drawings by Helene Carter, and published by Franklin Watts, Inc. This is a children's book, but contains so much information that young people and adults find it interesting.

HERE COME THE BEES! by Alice Goudey, published by Charles Scribner's Sons, illustrated with colored drawings by Garry MacKenzie, is for children seven to ten years of age.

THE YOUNG BEEKEEPER, by Harry McNicol, published by Frederick Warne & Co., tells of the experiences of a fifteen-year-old boy who went to live with his grandfather, a beekeeper, and had a thrilling experience caring for his own colony of bees.

THE WORLD OF THE HONEYBEE, by Colin G. Butler, published by The Macmillan Co. It contains eighty-seven black and white photographs and two in color. This is an adult book, but is written so that children who become fascinated by bees can read it.

A BOOK ABOUT BEES, by Edwin Way Teale, published by Indiana University Press, is illustrated with eighty-five photographs by the author. It gives a wide range of information about honeybees.

BEES, THEIR VISION, CHEMICAL SENSES, AND LANGUAGE, by Karl von Frisch, one of the great students of bees, is illustrated with photographs and drawings. It is published by Cornell University Press.

THE DANCING BEES, by Karl von Frisch, published by Harcourt, Brace & Co., gives more detailed information for the person who wishes to study bees thoroughly. Illustrated.

THE LIFE OF THE BEE, by Maurice Maeterlinck, is one of the classic books about bees. It is available in a paper-bound edition from The New American Library, and in a regular binding from Dodd, Mead & Co.

Lightning Source UK Ltd.
Milton Keynes UK
UKHW030002240223
417562UK00012B/60